AUSTIN RESTAURANT GUIDE 2018

RESTAURANTS, BARS & CAFES
★★★★☆

The Most Positively Reviewed and Recommended Restaurants in the City

AUSTIN RESTAURANT GUIDE 2018
Best Rated Restaurants in Austin, Texas

© Harris C. Haddock, 2018
© E.G.P. Editorial, 2018

Printed in USA.

ISBN-13: 978-1545052716
ISBN-10: 1545052719

Copyright © 2018
All rights reserved.

AUSTIN RESTAURANT GUIDE 2018
Most Recommended Restaurants in Austin

This directory is dedicated to Austin Business Owners and Managers who provide the experience that the locals and tourists enjoy. Thanks you very much for all that you do and thank for being the "People Choice".

Thanks to everyone that posts their reviews online and the amazing reviews sites that make our life easier.

The places listed in this book are the most positively reviewed and recommended by locals and travelers from around the world.

Thank you for your time and enjoy the directory that is designed with locals and tourist in mind!

TOP 500
RESTAURANTS
Ranked from #1 to #500

Austin Restaurant Guide 2018 / Restaurants, Bars & Cafés

#1
Hey!... You Gonna Eat or What?
Cuisines: Street Vendor, Southern, Food Truck
Average price: Inexpensive
Address: 1720 Barton Springs Rd
Austin, TX 78704
Phone: (512) 296-3547

#2
Troy
Cuisines: Turkish, Mediterranean
Average price: Inexpensive
Address: 8105 Mesa Dr
Austin, TX 78759
Phone: (512) 897-2860

#3
Stonehouse Wood Fire Grill
Cuisines: American, Mediterranean, Food Truck
Average price: Inexpensive
Address: 5400 Balcones Dr
Austin, TX 78731
Phone: (512) 769-6478

#4
Salty Sow
Cuisines: American, Gastropub
Average price: Modest
Address: 1917 Manor Rd
Austin, TX 78722
Phone: (512) 391-2337

#5
Moonshine Patio Bar & Grill
Cuisines: American, Southern, Breakfast & Brunch
Average price: Modest
Address: 303 Red River St
Austin, TX 78701
Phone: (512) 236-9599

#6
The Hightower
Cuisines: American
Average price: Modest
Address: 1209 E 7th St
Austin, TX 78702
Phone: (512) 524-1448

#7
Franklin Barbecue
Cuisines: Barbeque
Average price: Modest
Address: 900 E 11th St
Austin, TX 78702
Phone: (512) 653-1187

#8
Nutter Buster BBQ & Comfort
Cuisines: Food Truck, Barbeque, Comfort Food
Average price: Inexpensive
Address: 6218 Brodie Ln
Austin, TX 78749
Phone: (512) 903-9774

#9
Chicken Lollypop
Cuisines: Indian, Chinese, Vegetarian
Average price: Inexpensive
Address: 1005 E Braker Ln
Austin, TX 78753
Phone: (512) 909-9826

#10
Chago's
Cuisines: Puerto Rican
Average price: Modest
Address: 7301 N Lamar Blvd
Austin, TX 78752
Phone: (512) 275-6013

#11
Odd Duck
Cuisines: Restaurant
Average price: Expensive
Address: 1201 South Lamar Boulevard
Austin, TX 78704
Phone: (512) 433-6521

#12
Jacoby's Restaurant & Mercantile
Cuisines: American, Southern
Average price: Expensive
Address: 3235 E Cesar Chavez St
Austin, TX 78702
Phone: (512) 366-5808

#13
Kin and Comfort
Cuisines: Asian Fusion
Average price: Inexpensive
Address: 1700 W Parmer
Austin, TX 78727
Phone: (512) 832-7870

#14
Little Barrel and Brown
Cuisines: American
Average price: Modest
Address: 1716 S Congress Ave
Austin, TX 78704
Phone: (512) 582-1229

#15
Barley Swine
Cuisines: Gastropub, American
Average price: Expensive
Address: 2024 S Lamar Blvd
Austin, TX 78704
Phone: (512) 394-8150

#16
Melvin's Deli Comfort
Cuisines: Sandwiches, Deli, Food Truck
Average price: Inexpensive
Address: 501 E 53rd St
Austin, TX 78751
Phone: (512) 705-3906

#17
Republic of Sandwich
Cuisines: Deli, Sandwiches
Average price: Inexpensive
Address: 2320 Hancock Dr
Austin, TX 78756
Phone: (512) 960-6566

#18
Second Bar + Kitchen
Cuisines: American
Average price: Modest
Address: 200 Congress Ave
Austin, TX 78701
Phone: (512) 827-2750

#19
Jack Allen's Kitchen
Cuisines: American
Average price: Modest
Address: 7720 Hwy 71 W
Austin, TX 78735
Phone: (512) 852-8558

#20
Sonora Hot Dogs
Cuisines: Hot Dogs, Food Truck
Average price: Inexpensive
Address: 5715 Burnet Rd
Austin, TX 78756
Phone: (512) 994-8982

#21
Patrizi's
Cuisines: Italian, Food Stand
Average price: Modest
Address: 2307 Manor Rd
Austin, TX 78722
Phone: (512) 522-4834

#22
Ng BMT
Cuisines: Sandwiches, Desserts, Vietnamese
Average price: Inexpensive
Address: 8557 Research Blvd
Austin, TX 78758
Phone: (512) 931-1088

#23
Zoës Kitchen
Cuisines: Mediterranean
Average price: Inexpensive
Address: 5601 Brodie Ln
Austin, TX 78745
Phone: (512) 358-0888

#24
Porter Ale House & Gastropub
Cuisines: Gastropub
Average price: Modest
Address: 3715 S 1st St
Austin, TX 78704
Phone: (512) 291-6299

#25
Veracruz All Natural
Cuisines: Mexican, Food Truck
Average price: Inexpensive
Address: 1403 E 7th St
Austin, TX 78702
Phone: (512) 318-1830

#26
Gourdough's Public House
Cuisines: Pub, American
Average price: Modest
Address: 2700 S Lamar Blvd
Austin, TX 78704
Phone: (512) 912-9070

#27
Eastside Cafe
Cuisines: American
Average price: Modest
Address: 2113 Manor Rd
Austin, TX 78722
Phone: (512) 476-5858

#28
Salt & Time
Cuisines: Butcher, American
Average price: Modest
Address: 1912 E 7th St
Austin, TX 78702
Phone: (512) 524-1383

#29
Santorini Cafe
Cuisines: Greek, Wine Bar
Average price: Inexpensive
Address: 11800 N Lamar Blvd
Austin, TX 78753
Phone: (512) 833-6000

#30
Roaring Fork
Cuisines: American
Average price: Modest
Address: 701 Congress Ave
Austin, TX 78701
Phone: (512) 583-0000

#31
The Grub House
Cuisines: American, Food Stand
Average price: Inexpensive
Address: 7th and Red River St
Austin, TX 78701
Phone: (512) 900-9464

#33
The Grove
Cuisines: Pizza, Wine Bar
Average price: Modest
Address: 6317 Bee Caves Rd
Austin, TX 78746
Phone: (512) 327-8822

#32
Little Deli & Pizzeria
Cuisines: Deli, Pizza, Sandwiches
Average price: Inexpensive
Address: 7101-A Woodrow Ave
Austin, TX 78757
Phone: (512) 467-7402

#34
Ramen Tatsu-Ya
Cuisines: Ramen
Average price: Modest
Address: 8557 Research Blvd
Austin, TX 78758
Phone: (512) 834-8810

#35
Gourmands
Cuisines: Sandwiches, Deli, Gastropub
Average price: Inexpensive
Address: 2316 Webberville Rd
Austin, TX 78702
Phone: (512) 610-2031

#36
Tacodeli
Cuisines: Mexican, Vegetarian
Average price: Inexpensive
Address: 1500B Spyglass Dr
Austin, TX 78746
Phone: (512) 732-0303

#37
Josephine House
Cuisines: American
Average price: Modest
Address: 1601 Waterson Ave
Austin, TX 78703
Phone: (512) 477-5584

#38
Salata
Cuisines: Salad
Average price: Modest
Address: 10515 N Mopac Expy
Austin, TX 78759
Phone: (512) 487-5497

#39
Cabo Bobs Burritos
Cuisines: Mexican
Average price: Inexpensive
Address: 500 E Ben White Blvd
Austin, TX 78704
Phone: (512) 432-1111

#40
Fabi + Rosi
Cuisines: European, French, German
Average price: Modest
Address: 509 Hearn St
Austin, TX 78703
Phone: (512) 236-0642

#41
Justine's Brasserie
Cuisines: French
Average price: Modest
Address: 4710 E 5th St
Austin, TX 78702
Phone: (512) 385-2900

#42
Turf N' Surf Po Boy
Cuisines: Cajun, Creole, Food Stand, Seafood
Average price: Modest
Address: 407 Lavaca St
Austin, TX 78704
Phone: (512) 276-2763

#43
Fricano's Deli
Cuisines: Deli, Sandwiches
Average price: Inexpensive
Address: 2405 Nueces St
Austin, TX 78705
Phone: (512) 482-3322

#44
Valentina's Tex Mex BBQ
Cuisines: Barbeque, Tex-Mex, Mexican
Average price: Inexpensive
Address: 600 W 6th St
Austin, TX 78701
Phone: (512) 221-4248

#45
East Side King
Cuisines: Thai
Average price: Modest
Address: 2310 S Lamar Blvd
Austin, TX 78704
Phone: (512) 383-8382

#46
Dai Due Butcher Shop & Supper Club
Cuisines: Butcher, American
Average price: Modest
Address: 2406 Manor Rd
Austin, TX 78722
Phone: (512) 524-0688

#47
Easy Tiger
Cuisines: German, Bakery, American
Average price: Modest
Address: 709 E 6th St
Austin, TX 78701
Phone: (512) 614-4972

#48
la Barbecue
Cuisines: Barbeque, Food Truck
Average price: Modest
Address: 902 E Cesar Chavez
Austin, TX 78702
Phone: (512) 605-9696

#49
Noble Sandwich Co
Cuisines: Sandwiches
Average price: Inexpensive
Address: 4805 Burnet Rd
Austin, TX 78756
Phone: (512) 666-5124

#50
Licha's Cantina
Cuisines: Bar, Mexican, Gluten-Free
Average price: Modest
Address: 1306 E 6th St
Austin, TX 78702
Phone: (512) 480-5960

#51
Fork and Vine
Cuisines: American, Wine Bar
Average price: Expensive
Address: 3010 W Anderson Ln
Austin, TX 78757
Phone: (512) 489-7000

#52
Hi Hat Public House
Cuisines: American, Bar
Average price: Modest
Address: 2121 E 6th St
Austin, TX 78702
Phone: (512) 478-8700

#53
The Flying Carpet
Cuisines: Moroccan, Food Stand, Street Vendor
Average price: Inexpensive
Address: 504 W Oltorf
Austin, TX 78704
Phone: (512) 744-5651

#54
Luke's Inside Out
Cuisines: Sandwiches, Food Truck
Average price: Modest
Address: 1109 S Lamar Blvd
Austin, TX 78704
Phone: (512) 589-8883

#55
Barlata
Cuisines: Tapas Bar
Average price: Modest
Address: 1500 S Lamar Blvd
Austin, TX 78704
Phone: (512) 473-2211

#56
FoodHeads
Cuisines: Sandwiches, Café
Average price: Inexpensive
Address: 616 W 34th St
Austin, TX 78705
Phone: (512) 420-8400

Austin Restaurant Guide 2018 / Restaurants, Bars & Cafés

#57
South Congress Cafe
Cuisines: Breakfast & Brunch, American
Average price: Modest
Address: 1600 S Congress Ave
Austin, TX 78704
Phone: (512) 447-3905

#58
Gardner
Cuisines: American
Average price: Expensive
Address: 1914 E 6th St
Austin, TX 78702
Phone: (512) 354-1480

#59
Mary's Pop Shop
Cuisines: Gelato, Coffee, Tea, Café
Average price: Inexpensive
Address: 3209 Red River St
Austin, TX 78705
Phone: (512) 334-9460

#60
Joe's Place
Cuisines: American, Sandwiches
Average price: Inexpensive
Address: 1814 E Mlk Jr Blvd
Austin, TX 78723
Phone: (512) 472-3105

#61
Michi Ramen
Cuisines: Ramen
Average price: Modest
Address: 6519 N Lamar Blvd
Austin, TX 78752
Phone: (512) 386-1908

#62
Koriente
Cuisines: Asian Fusion, Vegetarian, Gluten-Free
Average price: Inexpensive
Address: 621 E 7th St
Austin, TX 78701
Phone: (512) 275-0852

#63
Peached Tortilla
Cuisines: Asian Fusion, Southern
Average price: Modest
Address: 5520 Burnet Rd
Austin, TX 78756
Phone: (512) 330-4439

#64
Javelina
Cuisines: American, Pub
Average price: Modest
Address: 69 Rainey St
Austin, TX 78701
Phone: (512) 382-6917

#65
Austin Daily Press
Cuisines: Deli, Sandwiches, Comfort Food
Average price: Inexpensive
Address: 1900 E Martin Luther King Blvd
Austin, TX 78702
Phone: (512) 828-6463

#66
Micklethwait Craft Meats
Cuisines: Barbeque
Average price: Modest
Address: 1309 Rosewood Ave
Austin, TX 78702
Phone: (512) 791-5961

#67
Independence Fine Foods
Cuisines: Sandwiches, Salad, Vegan
Average price: Modest
Address: 1807 W Slaughter Ln
Austin, TX 78748
Phone: (512) 363-5672

#68
Shhmaltz
Cuisines: Vegan, Food Truck, Deli
Average price: Inexpensive
Address: 913 E Cesar Chavez
Austin, TX 78702
Phone: (512) 529-1882

#69
Austin Beer Garden Brewing Company
Cuisines: Brewerie, Sandwiches, Pizza
Average price: Modest
Address: 1305 W Oltorf St
Austin, TX 78704
Phone: (512) 298-2242

#70
La Fruta Feliz
Cuisines: Mexican
Average price: Inexpensive
Address: 3124 Manor Rd
Austin, TX 78723
Phone: (512) 473-0037

#71
NeWorld Cafe
Cuisines: Sandwiches, American, Caterer
Average price: Inexpensive
Address: 3742 Far W Blvd
Austin, TX 78731
Phone: (512) 340-1404

#72
888 Pan Asian Restaurant
Cuisines: Vietnamese, Asian Fusion
Average price: Inexpensive
Address: 2400 E Oltorf St
Austin, TX 78741
Phone: (512) 448-4722

#73
Balkan Cafe & Grill
Cuisines: Ethnic Food, European
Average price: Modest
Address: 11800 N Lamar Blvd
Austin, TX 78753
Phone: (737) 703-5990

#74
Olamaie
Cuisines: Southern
Average price: Expensive
Address: 1610 San Antonio St
Austin, TX 78701
Phone: (512) 474-2796

#75
Galaxy Café
Cuisines: American
Average price: Inexpensive
Address: 1000 W Lynn St
Austin, TX 78703
Phone: (512) 478-3434

#76
NO VA Kitchen & Bar
Cuisines: Bar, American
Average price: Modest
Address: 87 Rainey St
Austin, TX 78701
Phone: (512) 382-5651

#77
Hopdoddy Burger Bar
Cuisines: Burgers
Average price: Modest
Address: 1400 S Congress Ave
Austin, TX 78704
Phone: (512) 243-7505

#78
Javi's Best of Tex-Mex
Cuisines: Tex-Mex
Average price: Inexpensive
Address: 7709 E Ben White Blvd
Austin, TX 78744
Phone: (512) 386-8329

#79
El Sapo
Cuisines: Burgers
Average price: Modest
Address: 1900 Manor Rd
Austin, TX 78722
Phone: (512) 366-5154

#80
Halal Bros
Cuisines: Middle Eastern, Halal
Average price: Inexpensive
Address: 2712a Guadalupe St
Austin, TX 78705
Phone: (512) 284-8105

#81
Three Little Pigs
Cuisines: Food Stand
Average price: Inexpensive
Address: 1209 Rosewood Ave
Austin, TX 78702
Phone: (512) 653-5088

#82
The Jalopy Rotisserie & Press
Cuisines: Sandwiches, American
Average price: Inexpensive
Address: 1502 San Antonio St
Austin, TX 78701
Phone: (512) 814-8557

#83
Hanabi
Cuisines: Sushi Bar
Average price: Modest
Address: 2525 W Anderson Ln
Austin, TX 78757
Phone: (512) 407-9000

#84
Saigon Le Vendeur
Cuisines: Food Truck, Vietnamese
Average price: Inexpensive
Address: 2404 E 7th St
Austin, TX 78702
Phone: (512) 351-6916

#85
Cow Bells
Cuisines: Burgers, Caterer, Food Truck
Average price: Inexpensive
Address: 1620 E Riverside Dr
Austin, TX 78741
Phone: (512) 576-8855

#86
Bufalina
Cuisines: Pizza, Italian
Average price: Modest
Address: 1519 E Cesar Chavez
Austin, TX 78702
Phone: (512) 524-2523

#87
Go Go Gourmet
Cuisines: American, Café
Average price: Inexpensive
Address: 104 E 31st St
Austin, TX 78705
Phone: (512) 589-6063

#88
Banger's Sausage House & Beer Garden
Cuisines: Pub, American
Average price: Modest
Address: 79 & 81 Rainey St
Austin, TX 78701
Phone: (512) 386-1656

#89
Sarah's Mediterranean Grill & Market
Cuisines: Greek, Grocery, Mediterranean, Ethnic Food
Average price: Inexpensive
Address: 5222 Burnet Rd
Austin, TX 78756
Phone: (512) 419-7605

#90
Contigo
Cuisines: Bar, American
Average price: Modest
Address: 2027 Anchor Ln
Austin, TX 78723
Phone: (512) 614-2260

#91
Stinson's
Cuisines: American, Cocktail Bar
Average price: Inexpensive
Address: 4416 Burnet Rd
Austin, TX 78756
Phone: (512) 968-4970

#92
District Kitchen & Cocktails
Cuisines: American, Bar, Seafood
Average price: Modest
Address: 5900 W Slaughter Ln
Austin, TX 78749
Phone: (512) 351-8436

#93
Garbo's Restaurant
Cuisines: Seafood
Average price: Modest
Address: 14735 Bratton Ln
Austin, TX 78728
Phone: (512) 350-9814

#94
360 Pizza
Cuisines: Pizza
Average price: Modest
Address: 6203 N Capital of Texas Hwy
Austin, TX 78731
Phone: (512) 428-4788

#95
The Backspace
Cuisines: Italian, Pizza
Average price: Modest
Address: 507 San Jacinto St
Austin, TX 78701
Phone: (512) 474-9899

#96
Gus's World Famous Fried Chicken
Cuisines: Chicken Wings, Soul Food
Average price: Inexpensive
Address: 117 San Jacinto
Austin, TX 78701
Phone: (512) 474-4877

#97
Mettle - East Austin Bistro
Cuisines: American, Breakfast & Brunch
Average price: Modest
Address: 507 Calles St
Austin, TX 78702
Phone: (512) 236-1022

#98
Bombay Dhaba
Cuisines: Food Truck, Indian
Average price: Inexpensive
Address: 1207 S 1st St
Austin, TX 78704
Phone: (737) 247-4323

#99
Hopfields
Cuisines: Pub, French, Gastropub
Average price: Modest
Address: 3110 Guadalupe St
Austin, TX 78705
Phone: (512) 537-0467

#100
Bouldin Creek Cafe
Cuisines: Breakfast & Brunch, Café, Vegan
Average price: Inexpensive
Address: 1900 S 1st St
Austin, TX 78704
Phone: (512) 416-1601

#101
Brisket Boy's Bar-B-Q
Cuisines: Food Truck, Barbeque
Average price: Inexpensive
Address: 1403 E 7th St
Austin, TX 78702
Phone: (512) 663-3649

#102
Via 313 Pizza
Cuisines: Pizza
Average price: Modest
Address: 1111B E 6th St
Austin, TX 78702
Phone: (512) 939-1927

#103
Fat Cactus
Cuisines: Tex-Mex, Food Truck
Average price: Inexpensive
Address: 1318 S Congress Ave
Austin, TX 78704
Phone: (512) 585-4967

#104
The Bonneville
Cuisines: American
Average price: Modest
Address: 202 W Cesar Chavez St
Austin, TX 78701
Phone: (512) 428-4643

#105
Food! Food!
Cuisines: Sandwiches
Average price: Modest
Address: 2727 Exposition Blvd
Austin, TX 78703
Phone: (512) 474-8515

#106
The Carillon
Cuisines: American
Average price: Expensive
Address: 1900 University Ave
Austin, TX 78705
Phone: (512) 404-3655

#107
Taco Joint
Cuisines: Mexican
Average price: Inexpensive
Address: 2807 San Jacinto Blvd
Austin, TX 78705
Phone: (512) 473-8223

#108
Winebelly
Cuisines: Tapas Bar, Wine Bar
Average price: Modest
Address: 519 W Oltorf St
Austin, TX 78704
Phone: (512) 487-1569

#109
Fishey Bizness Seafood Co
Cuisines: Fish & Chips, Seafood
Average price: Inexpensive
Address: 902 E Cesar Chavez St
Austin, TX 78702
Phone: (512) 605-7895

#110
Freedmen's
Cuisines: Barbeque, Bar
Average price: Modest
Address: 2402 San Gabriel St
Austin, TX 78705
Phone: (512) 220-0953

#111
Blue Dahlia Bistro
Cuisines: Breakfast & Brunch, French
Average price: Modest
Address: 1115 E 11th St
Austin, TX 78702
Phone: (512) 542-9542

#112
Olive & June
Cuisines: Italian
Average price: Expensive
Address: 3411 Glenview Ave
Austin, TX 78703
Phone: (512) 467-9898

#113
Love Balls
Cuisines: Japanese, Food Stand
Average price: Inexpensive
Address: 2908 Fruth St
Austin, TX 78705
Phone: (512) 765-6286

#114
Elaine's Pork and Pie
Cuisines: American
Average price: Inexpensive
Address: 2113 Manor Rd
Austin, TX 78722
Phone: (512) 494-1464

#115
Workhorse Bar
Cuisines: Dive Bar, American
Average price: Inexpensive
Address: 100 N Loop Blvd E
Austin, TX 78751
Phone: (512) 323-5700

#116
Cabo Bob's Burritos
Cuisines: Mexican
Average price: Inexpensive
Address: 2828 Rio Grande St
Austin, TX 78705
Phone: (512) 432-1112

#117
Pueblo Viejo
Cuisines: Mexican, Food Stand, Food Delivery Services
Average price: Inexpensive
Address: 907 E 6th St
Austin, TX 78702
Phone: (512) 373-6557

#118
Conscious Cravings
Cuisines: Vegetarian, Vegan, Gluten-Free
Average price: Inexpensive
Address: 5715 Burnet Rd
Austin, TX 78756
Phone: (512) 782-0546

#119
Southern Hospitality
Cuisines: Southern, Buffet
Average price: Inexpensive
Address: 6700 Middle Fiskville Rd
Austin, TX 78752
Phone: (512) 458-4679

#120
Roaring Fork
Cuisines: American
Average price: Expensive
Address: 10850 Stonelake Blvd
Austin, TX 78759
Phone: (512) 342-2700

#121
Wink
Cuisines: American, Vegetarian
Average price: Expensive
Address: 1014 N Lamar Blvd
Austin, TX 78703
Phone: (512) 482-8868

#122
Tacodeli
Cuisines: Mexican
Average price: Inexpensive
Address: 4200 N Lamar Blvd
Austin, TX 78756
Phone: (512) 419-1900

#123
Lucky's Puccias
Cuisines: Sandwiches, Food Stand, Street Vendor
Average price: Inexpensive
Address: 817 W 5th St
Austin, TX 78701
Phone: (512) 739-8785

#124
Torchy's Tacos
Cuisines: Tex-Mex, Food Stand
Average price: Inexpensive
Address: 1311 S 1st St
Austin, TX 78704
Phone: (512) 366-0537

#125
Habanero Mexican Cafe
Cuisines: Mexican, Tex-Mex
Average price: Inexpensive
Address: 501 W Oltorf St
Austin, TX 78704
Phone: (512) 416-0443

#126
Hopdoddy Burger Bar
Cuisines: Burgers
Average price: Modest
Address: 2438 W Anderson Ln
Austin, TX 78757
Phone: (512) 467-2337

Austin Restaurant Guide 2018 / Restaurants, Bars & Cafés

#127
El Alma
Cuisines: American, Mexican
Average price: Modest
Address: 1025 Barton Springs Rd
Austin, TX 78704
Phone: (512) 609-8923

#128
Papouli's Greek Grill
Cuisines: Greek
Average price: Modest
Address: 1000 E 41st St
Austin, TX 78751
Phone: (512) 371-8811

#129
Regal Ravioli
Cuisines: Food Stand, Italian
Average price: Modest
Address: 1502 S 1st St
Austin, TX 78704
Phone: (512) 364-9752

#130
Black Star Co-op Pub & Brewery
Cuisines: Brewerie, Gastropub
Average price: Modest
Address: 7020 Easy Wind Dr
Austin, TX 78752
Phone: (512) 452-2337

#131
Arpeggio Grill
Cuisines: Pizza, Greek, Mediterranean
Average price: Inexpensive
Address: 6619 Airport Blvd
Austin, TX 78752
Phone: (512) 419-0110

#132
Burrito Factory
Cuisines: Mexican
Average price: Inexpensive
Address: 2025 Guadalupe St
Austin, TX 78705
Phone: (512) 227-5060

#133
Brass House
Cuisines: Lounge, Jazz, Blues, Italian
Average price: Modest
Address: 115 San Jacinto Blvd
Austin, TX 78701
Phone: (512) 296-2188

#134
Wholly Cow
Cuisines: Burgers
Average price: Inexpensive
Address: 3010 S Lamar Blvd
Austin, TX 78704
Phone: (512) 394-8156

#135
Taco Flats
Cuisines: Tex-Mex, Mexican, Bar
Average price: Modest
Address: 5520 Burnet Rd
Austin, TX 78756
Phone: (512) 619-9848

#136
Kome Sushi Kitchen
Cuisines: Japanese, Sushi Bar
Average price: Modest
Address: 4917 Airport Blvd
Austin, TX 78751
Phone: (512) 712-5700

#137
Counter Culture
Cuisines: Vegan, Vegetarian, Breakfast & Brunch
Average price: Inexpensive
Address: 2337 E Cesar Chavez St
Austin, TX 78702
Phone: (512) 524-1540

#138
The Mediterranean Chef
Cuisines: Ethnic Food, Mediterranean
Average price: Inexpensive
Address: 5908 Aurora Dr
Austin, TX 78757
Phone: (512) 970-9150

#139
Buenos Aires Café
Cuisines: Argentine
Average price: Modest
Address: 1201 E 6th St
Austin, TX 78702
Phone: (512) 382-1189

#140
Xian Sushi and Noodle
Cuisines: Japanese, Sushi Bar, Chinese
Average price: Modest
Address: 1801 E 51 St
Austin, TX 78723
Phone: (512) 469-7878

Austin Restaurant Guide 2018 / Restaurants, Bars & Cafés

#141
Swift's Attic
Cuisines: American, Gastropub, Vegetarian
Average price: Expensive
Address: 315 Congress Ave
Austin, TX 78701
Phone: (512) 482-8200

#142
Julie's Handmade Noodles
Cuisines: Chinese, Asian Fusion, Food Truck
Average price: Inexpensive
Address: 2512 Rio Grande St
Austin, TX 78705
Phone: (646) 508-3303

#143
Lamberts Downtown Barbecue
Cuisines: Barbeque, Breakfast & Brunch
Average price: Modest
Address: 401 W 2nd St
Austin, TX 78701
Phone: (512) 494-1500

#144
Maoz Vegetarian
Cuisines: Vegetarian, Middle Eastern
Average price: Inexpensive
Address: 4601 N Lamar Blvd
Austin, TX 78751
Phone: (512) 323-2259

#145
Tan My Restaurant
Cuisines: Vietnamese
Average price: Inexpensive
Address: 1601 Ohlen Rd
Austin, TX 78758
Phone: (512) 832-9585

#146
Sway
Cuisines: Thai, Asian Fusion
Average price: Expensive
Address: 1417 S 1st St
Austin, TX 78704
Phone: (512) 326-1999

#147
Pinthouse Pizza
Cuisines: Pizza, Brewerie
Average price: Modest
Address: 4729 Burnet Rd
Austin, TX 78756
Phone: (512) 436-9605

#148
Cuban Sandwich Cafe
Cuisines: Cuban, Bakery, Sandwiches
Average price: Inexpensive
Address: 1804 Briarcliff Blvd
Austin, TX 78723
Phone: (512) 501-6651

#149
Taqueria Mi Trailita
Cuisines: Food Truck, Mexican
Average price: Inexpensive
Address: 5301 Manor Rd
Austin, TX 78723
Phone: (512) 497-9877

#150
Frank
Cuisines: Hot Dogs, Lounge
Average price: Modest
Address: 407 Colorado St
Austin, TX 78701
Phone: (512) 494-6916

#151
VertsKebap
Cuisines: German, Sandwiches
Average price: Inexpensive
Address: 1500 S Lamar Blvd
Austin, TX 78704
Phone: (512) 382-6814

#152
Blake's on Sixth Street
Cuisines: Café
Average price: Modest
Address: 1221 W 6th St
Austin, TX 78703
Phone: (512) 215-0317

#153
Hula Hut
Cuisines: Tex-Mex, Hawaiian, Mexican
Average price: Modest
Address: 3825 Lake Austin Blvd
Austin, TX 78703
Phone: (512) 476-4852

#154
French Quarter Grille
Cuisines: American, Cajun, Creole
Average price: Modest
Address: 13000 N IH 35
Austin, TX 78753
Phone: (512) 832-9090

#155
Marye's Gourmet Pizza
Cuisines: Pizza, Salad, Sandwiches
Average price: Modest
Address: 3663 Bee Cave Rd
Austin, TX 78746
Phone: (512) 327-5222

#156
Yellow Jacket Social Club
Cuisines: Lounge, American
Average price: Inexpensive
Address: 1704 E 5th St
Austin, TX 78702
Phone: (512) 480-9572

#157
Stiles Switch BBQ & Brew
Cuisines: Barbeque
Average price: Modest
Address: 6610 N Lamar Blvd
Austin, TX 78757
Phone: (512) 380-9199

#158
Péché
Cuisines: Lounge, French, Cocktail Bar
Average price: Modest
Address: 208 W 4th St
Austin, TX 78701
Phone: (512) 494-4011

#159
Donut 7
Cuisines: Donuts, Breakfast & Brunch, Coffee, Tea
Average price: Inexpensive
Address: 11005 Burnet Rd
Austin, TX 78758
Phone: (512) 837-9221

#160
Wasota African Cuisine
Cuisines: African
Average price: Inexpensive
Address: 2323 S Lamar Blvd
Austin, TX 78704
Phone: (512) 565-3864

#161
Casa De Luz
Cuisines: Vegetarian, Vegan,
Average price: Modest
Address: 1701 Toomey Rd
Austin, TX 78704
Phone: (512) 476-2535

#162
Slab BBQ
Cuisines: American, Barbeque
Average price: Inexpensive
Address: 9012 Research Blvd
Austin, TX 78758
Phone: (512) 351-9977

#163
Counter Cafe East
Cuisines: Breakfast & Brunch, Diner, Burgers
Average price: Modest
Address: 1914 E 6th St
Austin, TX 78702
Phone: (512) 351-9961

#164
Kerbey Lane Cafe
Cuisines: Breakfast & Brunch, Café, American
Average price: Modest
Address: 3704 Kerbey Ln
Austin, TX 78731
Phone: (512) 451-1436

#165
Bartlett's
Cuisines: Steakhouse, American, Gluten-Free
Average price: Expensive
Address: 2408 W Anderson Ln
Austin, TX 78757
Phone: (512) 451-7333

#166
Qui
Cuisines: American
Average price: Exclusive
Address: 1600 E 6th St
Austin, TX 78702
Phone: (512) 436-9626

#167
Home Slice Pizza
Cuisines: Pizza, Sandwiches
Average price: Modest
Address: 1415 S Congress St
Austin, TX 78704
Phone: (512) 444-7437

#168
Cenote
Cuisines: Coffee, Tea, Café, American
Average price: Inexpensive
Address: 1010 E Cesar Chavez St
Austin, TX 78702
Phone: (512) 524-1311

#169
Corona Cafe
Cuisines: Coffee, Tea, Café
Average price: Inexpensive
Address: 1215 Corona Dr
Austin, TX 78723
Phone: (512) 524-0014

#170
Rockaway Beach ATX
Cuisines: Shaved Ice, Sandwiches, Hot Dogs
Average price: Inexpensive
Address: 1620 E Riverside Dr
Austin, TX 78741
Phone: (512) 550-4671

#171
El Regio
Cuisines: Mexican
Average price: Inexpensive
Address: 6615 Berkman Dr
Austin, TX 78723
Phone: (512) 933-9557

#172
Churro Co.
Cuisines: Desserts, Mexican, Food Truck
Average price: Inexpensive
Address: 1620 E. Riverside
Austin, TX 78702
Phone: (512) 905-5267

#173
Sawyer & Co
Cuisines: Cajun, Creole, Diner, Seafood
Average price: Modest
Address: 4827 E Cesar Chavez
Austin, TX 78702
Phone: (512) 531-9033

#174
Torchy's Tacos
Cuisines: Tex-Mex, Mexican, Breakfast & Brunch
Average price: Inexpensive
Address: 2801 Guadalupe St
Austin, TX 78705
Phone: (512) 494-8226

#175
Torchy's Tacos
Cuisines: Mexican, Tex-Mex, Breakfast & Brunch
Average price: Inexpensive
Address: 4211 Spicewood Springs Rd
Austin, TX 78731
Phone: (512) 291-7277

#176
Tapas Bravas
Cuisines: Spanish, Food Stand, Tapas
Average price: Modest
Address: 75 Rainey St
Austin, TX 78701
Phone: (512) 827-8479

#177
Vino Vino
Cuisines: Wine Bar, American
Average price: Modest
Address: 4119 Guadalupe St
Austin, TX 78751
Phone: (512) 465-9282

#178
Scotty's BBQ
Cuisines: Barbeque, Food Truck, Food Delivery Services
Average price: Inexpensive
Address: 74 Rainey St
Austin, TX 78702
Phone: (512) 350-1615

#179
Êpicerie Cafe & Grocery
Cuisines: Grocery, Café
Average price: Modest
Address: 2307 Hancock Dr
Austin, TX 78756
Phone: (512) 371-6840

#180
St Philip Pizza Parlor + Bakeshop
Cuisines: Pizza, Bakery, Breakfast & Brunch
Average price: Modest
Address: 4715 S Lamar Blvd
Austin, TX 78745
Phone: (512) 358-7445

#181
Bacon
Cuisines: American, Breakfast & Brunch
Average price: Modest
Address: 900 W 10th St
Austin, TX 78703
Phone: (512) 322-9777

#182
Pour House Pints And Pies
Cuisines: Pizza, Pub
Average price: Modest
Address: 11835 Jollyville Rd
Austin, TX 78759
Phone: (512) 270-4740

#183
Searsucker
Cuisines: American
Average price: Expensive
Address: 415 Colorado St
Austin, TX 78701
Phone: (512) 394-8000

#184
Supper Friends
Cuisines: Diner
Average price: Expensive
Address: 3012 Gonzales St
Austin, TX 78702
Phone: (512) 385-6700

#185
Cuban Sandwich Cafe
Cuisines: Cuban, Café, Sandwiches
Average price: Inexpensive
Address: 9616 N Lamar Blvd
Austin, TX 78723
Phone: (512) 669-5242

#186
Henri's
Cuisines: Cheese Shop, Wine Bar, American
Average price: Modest
Address: 2026 S Lamar Blvd
Austin, TX 78704
Phone: (512) 442-3373

#187
Teriyaki Madness
Cuisines: Japanese, Hawaiian, Asian Fusion
Average price: Inexpensive
Address: 7301 Burnet Rd
Austin, TX 78757
Phone: (512) 300-0386

#188
Slake Cafe
Cuisines: Café, American
Average price: Inexpensive
Address: 120 E 7th St
Austin, TX 78701
Phone: (512) 476-0060

#189
Kebabalicious
Cuisines: Turkish, Food Truck
Average price: Inexpensive
Address: 1720 Barton Springs Rd
Austin, TX 78704
Phone: (512) 468-1065

#190
Austin Terrier
Cuisines: Sandwiches, Pizza
Average price: Inexpensive
Address: 3435 Greystone Dr
Austin, TX 78731
Phone: (512) 369-3751

#191
Sweetwater
Cuisines: Jazz, Blues, Music Venues, Cajun, Creole
Average price: Inexpensive
Address: 730 W Stassney Ln
Austin, TX 78745
Phone: (512) 270-9993

#192
Mulberry
Cuisines: Wine Bar, American
Average price: Modest
Address: 360 Nueces St
Austin, TX 78701
Phone: (512) 320-0297

#193
Magnolia Cafe
Cuisines: Breakfast & Brunch, American, Tex-Mex
Average price: Inexpensive
Address: 1920 S Congress Ave
Austin, TX 78704
Phone: (512) 445-0000

#194
Kyōten
Cuisines: Japanese, Food Stand
Average price: Modest
Address: 1211 E 6th
Austin, TX 78702
Phone: (512) 888-7559

#195
Torchy's Tacos
Cuisines: Mexican, Tex-Mex
Average price: Inexpensive
Address: 2809 S 1st St
Austin, TX 78704
Phone: (512) 444-0300

#196
Arro
Cuisines: French
Average price: Expensive
Address: 601 W 6th St
Austin, TX 78701
Phone: (512) 992-2776

#197
Baton Creole
Cuisines: Food Truck, Cajun, Creole, Gluten-Free
Average price: Inexpensive
Address: 1104 E 6th St
Austin, TX 78702
Phone: (512) 434-0671

#198
VertsKebap
Cuisines: Mediterranean, Sandwiches
Average price: Inexpensive
Address: 1801 E 51st St
Austin, TX 78723
Phone: (512) 373-8736

#199
Blue Ox BBQ
Cuisines: Barbeque
Average price: Modest
Address: 1505 Town Creek Dr
Austin, TX 78741
Phone: (512) 537-2047

#200
Drink Well
Cuisines: Gastropub, Bar, American
Average price: Modest
Address: 207 E 53rd St
Austin, TX 78751
Phone: (512) 614-6683

#201
Art of Tacos
Cuisines: Mexican, Food Truck
Average price: Inexpensive
Address: 75 Rainey St
Austin, TX 78701
Phone: (512) 666-8226

#202
Hot Mama's Cafe
Cuisines: Coffee, Tea, Mediterranean
Average price: Inexpensive
Address: 2401 E 6th St, Ste 1004
Austin, TX 78702
Phone: (512) 476-6262

#203
Haymaker
Cuisines: American, Sandwiches
Average price: Modest
Address: 2310 Manor Rd
Austin, TX 78722
Phone: (512) 243-6702

#204
The Clay Pit
Cuisines: Indian
Average price: Modest
Address: 1601 Guadalupe St
Austin, TX 78701
Phone: (512) 322-5131

#205
Taco More
Cuisines: Mexican, Tex-Mex
Average price: Inexpensive
Address: 9414 Parkfield Dr
Austin, TX 78758
Phone: (512) 821-1561

#206
East Side King @ Liberty Bar
Cuisines: Asian Fusion, Food Stand, Food Truck
Average price: Inexpensive
Address: 1618 1/2 E 6th St
Austin, TX 78702
Phone: (512) 422-5884

#207
Hoboken Pie
Cuisines: Pizza
Average price: Inexpensive
Address: 718 Red River St
Austin, TX 78701
Phone: (512) 477-4256

#208
Taco N' Madre
Cuisines: Mexican, Food Stand
Average price: Inexpensive
Address: 628 E Oltorf St
Austin, TX 78704
Phone: (512) 547-7996

#209
Magnolia Cafe
Cuisines: American, Breakfast & Brunch
Average price: Inexpensive
Address: 2304 Lake Austin Blvd
Austin, TX 78703
Phone: (512) 478-8645

#210
La Cocina de Consuelo
Cuisines: Mexican, Breakfast & Brunch
Average price: Inexpensive
Address: 4516 Burnet Rd
Austin, TX 78756
Phone: (512) 524-4740

#211
Foreign & Domestic
Cuisines: American
Average price: Modest
Address: 306 E 53rd St
Austin, TX 78751
Phone: (512) 459-1010

#212
Paco's Tacos
Cuisines: Mexican
Average price: Inexpensive
Address: 1304 E 51st St
Austin, TX 78723
Phone: (512) 323-6206

#213
Café Crème
Cuisines: Coffee, Tea, Bakery, Café
Average price: Inexpensive
Address: 1834 E Oltorf St
Austin, TX 78741
Phone: (512) 448-9473

#214
The Jackalope
Cuisines: Dive Bar, Burgers, Pizza
Average price: Inexpensive
Address: 404 E 6th St
Austin, TX 78701
Phone: (512) 472-3663

#215
Arlo's
Cuisines: Vegan, Vegetarian, Food Truck
Average price: Inexpensive
Address: 900 Red River St
Austin, TX 78702
Phone: (512) 402-2667

#216
Apothecary Cafe & Wine Bar
Cuisines: Wine Bar, American
Average price: Modest
Address: 4800 Burnet Rd
Austin, TX 78756
Phone: (512) 371-1600

#217
Thanh Nhi
Cuisines: Vietnamese
Average price: Inexpensive
Address: 9200 N Lamar Blvd
Austin, TX 78753
Phone: (512) 834-1736

#218
JR'S Tacos
Cuisines: Mexican
Average price: Inexpensive
Address: 1921 Cedar Bend Dr
Austin, TX 78757
Phone: (512) 831-5554

#219
Café Java
Cuisines: Coffee, Tea, Breakfast & Brunch
Average price: Inexpensive
Address: 11900 Metric Blvd
Austin, TX 78758
Phone: (512) 339-7677

#220
House Pizzeria
Cuisines: Pizza
Average price: Modest
Address: 5111 Airport Blvd
Austin, TX 78751
Phone: (512) 600-4999

#221
Inka Chicken
Cuisines: Peruvian, Fast Food, Latin American
Average price: Inexpensive
Address: 1707 Wells Branch Pkwy
Austin, TX 78728
Phone: (512) 252-2222

#222
Asiana Indian Cuisine
Cuisines: Indian
Average price: Modest
Address: 801 E William Cannon Dr
Austin, TX 78745
Phone: (512) 445-3435

#223
Conscious Cravings
Cuisines: Gluten-Free, Vegan, Vegetarian
Average price: Inexpensive
Address: 1311 S 1st St
Austin, TX 78704
Phone: (512) 582-9182

#224
La Traviata
Cuisines: Italian
Average price: Modest
Address: 314 Congress Ave
Austin, TX 78701
Phone: (512) 479-8131

#225
Big Fat Greek Gyros
Cuisines: Street Vendor, Greek
Average price: Inexpensive
Address: 74 Rainey St
Austin, TX 78701
Phone: (512) 626-1277

#226
Country Boyz Fixns
Cuisines: American
Average price: Inexpensive
Address: 4140 E 12th S
Austin, TX 78721
Phone: (512) 928-5555

#227
Torchy's Tacos
Cuisines: Tex-Mex, Mexican, Breakfast & Brunch
Average price: Inexpensive
Address: 1801 E 51 St
Austin, TX 78723
Phone: (512) 322-2411

#228
laV
Cuisines: French, Bar
Average price: Expensive
Address: 1501 E 7th St
Austin, TX 78702
Phone: (512) 391-1888

#229
Sao Paulo's Restaurant
Cuisines: Brazilian, Tex-Mex
Average price: Modest
Address: 2809 San Jacinto Blvd
Austin, TX 78705
Phone: (512) 473-9988

#230
Lucky Robot
Cuisines: Japanese, Sushi Bar, Breakfast & Brunch
Average price: Modest
Address: 1303 S Congress
Austin, TX 78704
Phone: (512) 444-8081

#231
Restaurant Jezebel
Cuisines: American, French
Average price: Exclusive
Address: 800 W 6th St
Austin, TX 78701
Phone: (512) 436-9643

#232
Shady Grove
Cuisines: American, Tex-Mex, Bar
Average price: Modest
Address: 1624 Barton Springs Rd
Austin, TX 78704
Phone: (512) 474-9991

#233
Due Forni
Cuisines: Pizza, Italian
Average price: Modest
Address: 106 E 6th St
Austin, TX 78701
Phone: (512) 391-9300

#234
Azul Tequila
Cuisines: Mexican
Average price: Modest
Address: 3815 Dry Creek Dr
Austin, TX 78731
Phone: (512) 334-9973

#235
Kebabalicious
Cuisines: Turkish
Average price: Inexpensive
Address: 1311 E 7th St
Austin, TX 78702
Phone: (512) 394-6562

#236
Rudy's Country Store & Bar-B-Q
Cuisines: Barbeque, Fast Food
Average price: Modest
Address: 2451 S Capital of Texas Hwy
Austin, TX 78746
Phone: (512) 329-5554

#237
Old School Bar & Grill
Cuisines: American, Burgers
Average price: Modest
Address: 401 E 6th St
Austin, TX 78701
Phone: (512) 722-6351

#238
Abel's On the Lake
Cuisines: Breakfast & Brunch, Bar, American
Average price: Modest
Address: 3826 Lake Austin Blvd
Austin, TX 78703
Phone: (512) 904-0570

#239
Peace Bakery and Deli
Cuisines: Mediterranean, Middle Eastern, Desserts
Average price: Inexpensive
Address: 11220 N Lamar Blvd
Austin, TX 78753
Phone: (512) 386-1152

#240
24 Diner
Cuisines: Diner, American
Average price: Modest
Address: 600 N Lamar Blvd
Austin, TX 78703
Phone: (512) 472-5400

#241
Delicious Thai
Cuisines: Food Truck, Thai
Average price: Inexpensive
Address: 411 W 23rd St
Austin, TX 78705
Phone: (512) 888-6189

#242
Uchi
Cuisines: Sushi Bar, Japanese
Average price: Exclusive
Address: 801 S Lamar Blvd
Austin, TX 78704
Phone: (512) 916-4808

#243
East Side Pies
Cuisines: Pizza
Average price: Inexpensive
Address: 1401 B Rosewood Ave
Austin, TX 78702
Phone: (512) 524-0933

#244
Nubian Queen Lola's Cajun Soul Food
Cuisines: Cajun, Creole, Soul Food
Average price: Inexpensive
Address: 1815 Rosewood Ave
Austin, TX 78702
Phone: (512) 474-5652

#245
Kebabalicious
Cuisines: Turkish
Average price: Inexpensive
Address: 7th St & Congress Ave
Austin, TX 78701
Phone: (512) 468-1065

#246
The Silo on 7th
Cuisines: Burgers, Bar
Average price: Modest
Address: 1300 E 7th St
Austin, TX 78702
Phone: (512) 524-0866

#247
North Italia
Cuisines: Italian, Pizza
Average price: Modest
Address: 11506 Century Oaks Ter
Austin, TX 78758
Phone: (512) 339-4400

#248
Mi Madre's
Cuisines: Tex-Mex, Breakfast & Brunch
Average price: Inexpensive
Address: 2201 Manor Rd
Austin, TX 78722
Phone: (512) 322-9721

#249
VertsKebap
Cuisines: Sandwiches, Mediterranean
Average price: Inexpensive
Address: 2530 Guadalupe St
Austin, TX 78705
Phone: (512) 215-9589

#250
Juan In A Million
Cuisines: Mexican
Average price: Inexpensive
Address: 2300 E Cesar Chavez St
Austin, TX 78702
Phone: (512) 472-3872

#251
Tamale House East
Cuisines: Mexican
Average price: Inexpensive
Address: 1707 E 6th St
Austin, TX 78702
Phone: (512) 495-9504

#252
Whip In
Cuisines: Indian, Grocery, Bar
Average price: Modest
Address: 1950 Hwy 35 S
Austin, TX 78704
Phone: (512) 442-5337

#253
Lebowski's Grill
Cuisines: Burgers
Average price: Inexpensive
Address: 8909 Burnet Rd
Austin, TX 78757
Phone: (512) 419-7166

#254
Top Notch
Cuisines: Fast Food, Burgers
Average price: Inexpensive
Address: 7525 Burnet Rd
Austin, TX 78757
Phone: (512) 452-2181

#255
NeWorlDeli
Cuisines: Deli, Sandwiches
Average price: Inexpensive
Address: 4101 Guadalupe St
Austin, TX 78751
Phone: (512) 451-7170

#256
Driskill Bar
Cuisines: Lounge, American, Cocktail Bar
Average price: Modest
Address: 604 Brazos St
Austin, TX 78701
Phone: (512) 391-7162

#257
Billy's on Burnet
Cuisines: American, Pub
Average price: Inexpensive
Address: 2105 Hancock Dr
Austin, TX 78756
Phone: (512) 407-9305

#258
Marakesh Cafe & Grill
Cuisines: Mediterranean, Middle Eastern, Greek
Average price: Modest
Address: 3301 Steck Ave
Austin, TX 78757
Phone: (512) 476-7735

#259
Picnik Austin
Cuisines: Coffee, Gluten-Free, Juice Bar
Average price: Modest
Address: 1700 S Lamar Blvd
Austin, TX 78704
Phone: (512) 293-6118

#260
The Austin Club
Cuisines: American
Average price: Expensive
Address: 110 E 9th St
Austin, TX 78701
Phone: (512) 477-9496

#261
Dos Batos - Woodfired Tacos
Cuisines: Mexican
Average price: Inexpensive
Address: 2525 W Anderson Ln
Austin, TX 78757
Phone: (512) 452-0001

#262
Dock & Roll Diner
Cuisines: Food Stand, Sandwiches
Average price: Modest
Address: 1503 S 1st St
Austin, TX 78704
Phone: (512) 924-1766

#263
The Vegan Nom
Cuisines: Mexican, Food Stand, Vegan
Average price: Inexpensive
Address: 120 E N Loop Blvd
Austin, TX 78751
Phone: (512) 217-7257

#264
The Mean Eyed Cat
Cuisines: Music Venues, Barbeque
Average price: Inexpensive
Address: 1621 W 5th St
Austin, TX 78703
Phone: (512) 920-6645

#265
Hao-Q Asian Kitchen
Cuisines: Chinese, Vietnamese
Average price: Modest
Address: 3742 Far W Blvd
Austin, TX 78731
Phone: (512) 338-6003

#266
Parkside
Cuisines: Seafood, American
Average price: Expensive
Address: 301 E 6th St
Austin, TX 78701
Phone: (512) 474-9898

#267
Galaxy Cafe
Cuisines: American
Average price: Modest
Address: 4616 Triangle Ave
Austin, TX 78705
Phone: (512) 323-9494

#268
Tacodeli
Cuisines: Mexican, Deli
Average price: Inexpensive
Address: 12001 N Burnet Rd
Austin, TX 78758
Phone: (512) 339-1700

#269
The Original New Orleans Po-boy And Gumbo Shop
Cuisines: Cajun, Creole, Sandwiches
Average price: Modest
Address: 1701 E Cesar Chavez St
Austin, TX 78702
Phone: (512) 406-9237

#270
Brunch Haus
Cuisines: Food Truck, Southern, Breakfast & Brunch
Average price: Inexpensive
Address: 415 Jessie St
Austin, TX 78704
Phone: (512) 962-9616

#271
360 Uno Trattoria & Wine Bar
Cuisines: Italian, Pizza
Average price: Modest
Address: 3801 Capitol of Texas Hwy N, Ste G-100 Austin, TX 78746
Phone: (512) 327-5505

#272
Casino El Camino
Cuisines: American, Cocktail Bar
Average price: Inexpensive
Address: 517 E 6th St
Austin, TX 78701
Phone: (512) 469-9330

#273
BuzzMill Coffee
Cuisines: Coffee, Tea, Lounge, Barbeque
Average price: Inexpensive
Address: 1505 Town Creek Dr
Austin, TX 78741
Phone: (512) 912-9221

#274
Bar Congress
Cuisines: American, Lounge
Average price: Modest
Address: 200 Congress Ave
Austin, TX 78701
Phone: (512) 827-2760

#275
Chuy's
Cuisines: Tex-Mex
Average price: Modest
Address: 1728 Barton Springs Rd
Austin, TX 78704
Phone: (512) 474-4452

#276
Texas Chili Parlor
Cuisines: American, Bar
Average price: Inexpensive
Address: 1409 Lavaca St
Austin, TX 78701
Phone: (512) 472-2828

#277
Skinny Limits
Cuisines: Food Truck, Juice Bar, Vegetarian
Average price: Inexpensive
Address: 2201 Lake Austin Blvd
Austin, TX 78703
Phone: (512) 689-6269

#278
Tucci's Southside Subs
Cuisines: Sandwiches
Average price: Inexpensive
Address: 801 E William Cannon Dr
Austin, TX 78745
Phone: (512) 440-1850

#279
Z'Tejas Southwestern Grill
Cuisines: Tex-Mex, Mexican
Average price: Modest
Address: 1110 W 6th St
Austin, TX 78703
Phone: (512) 478-5355

#280
North By Northwest Restaurant & Brewery
Cuisines: Brewerie, American, Gluten-Free
Average price: Modest
Address: 10010 N Capital Of Texas Hwy
Austin, TX 78759
Phone: (512) 467-6969

#281
Zed's
Cuisines: American
Average price: Modest
Address: 501 Canyon Ridge Dr
Austin, TX 78753
Phone: (512) 339-9337

#282
Julio's Café
Cuisines: Mexican
Average price: Inexpensive
Address: 4230 Duval St
Austin, TX 78751
Phone: (512) 452-1040

#283
CRAVE
Cuisines: American, Sushi Bar
Average price: Modest
Address: 340 E 2nd St
Austin, TX 78701
Phone: (512) 469-0000

#284
Live Oak Market
Cuisines: Coffee, Tea, Sandwiches, Convenience Store
Average price: Inexpensive
Address: 4410 Manchaca Rd
Austin, TX 78745
Phone: (512) 416-0300

#285
Snap Kitchen
Cuisines: American, Gluten-Free, Vegetarian
Average price: Modest
Address: 10001 Research Blvd
Austin, TX 78759
Phone: (512) 346-5959

#286
El Primo
Cuisines: Mexican, Food Stand
Average price: Inexpensive
Address: 2101 S 1st St
Austin, TX 78704
Phone: (512) 227-5060

#287
Super Burrito
Cuisines: Mexican
Average price: Inexpensive
Address: 1800 E Oltorf St
Austin, TX 78741
Phone: (512) 443-8226

#288
Papalote Taco House
Cuisines: Mexican
Average price: Inexpensive
Address: 2803 S Lamar Blvd
Austin, TX 78704
Phone: (512) 804-2474

#289
Blue Dahlia Bistro
Cuisines: Café, French
Average price: Modest
Address: 3663 Bee Caves Rd
Austin, TX 78746
Phone: (512) 306-1668

#290
Hyde Park Bar & Grill Central
Cuisines: American, Bar
Average price: Modest
Address: 4206 Duval St
Austin, TX 78751
Phone: (512) 458-3168

#291
Botticelli's
Cuisines: Italian
Average price: Modest
Address: 1321 S Congress Ave
Austin, TX 78704
Phone: (512) 916-1315

#292
Tarka Indian Kitchen
Cuisines: Indian, Gluten-Free, Vegetarian
Average price: Inexpensive
Address: 2525 W Anderson Ln
Austin, TX 78757
Phone: (512) 323-0955

#293
Hillside Farmacy
Cuisines: Diner, American, Breakfast & Brunch
Average price: Modest
Address: 1209 E 11th St
Austin, TX 78702
Phone: (512) 628-0168

#294
Tommy Want Wingy
Cuisines: Chicken Wings, Food Truck
Average price: Inexpensive
Address: 601 W Live Oak
Austin, TX 78704
Phone: (512) 662-8516

Austin Restaurant Guide 2018 / Restaurants, Bars & Cafés

#295
Rice Bowl Cafe
Cuisines: Chinese, Taiwanese
Average price: Inexpensive
Address: 11220 N Lamar Blvd
Austin, TX 78753
Phone: (512) 835-8888

#296
Fork & Taco
Cuisines: Mexican
Average price: Modest
Address: 4801 Burnet Rd
Austin, TX 78756
Phone: (512) 838-6768

#297
Pappadeaux Seafood Kitchen
Cuisines: Seafood, Cajun, Creole
Average price: Modest
Address: 6319 I-35 N
Austin, TX 78752
Phone: (512) 452-9363

#298
Elizabeth Street Cafe
Cuisines: Vietnamese, French
Average price: Modest
Address: 1501 S 1st St
Austin, TX 78704
Phone: (512) 291-2881

#299
San Francisco Bakery & Café
Cuisines: Sandwiches, Bakery
Average price: Inexpensive
Address: 2900 W Anderson Ln
Austin, TX 78757
Phone: (512) 302-3420

#300
Perla's
Cuisines: Seafood, Breakfast & Brunch
Average price: Expensive
Address: 1400 S Congress Ave
Austin, TX 78704
Phone: (512) 291-7300

#301
Goldis Sausage Company
Cuisines: Food Truck, Butcher, Barbeque
Average price: Inexpensive
Address: 1207 S 1st St
Austin, TX 78704
Phone: (512) 842-7714

#302
Clark's Oyster Bar
Cuisines: Seafood
Average price: Expensive
Address: 1200 W 6th St
Austin, TX 78703
Phone: (512) 297-2525

#303
Taco More
Cuisines: Mexican
Average price: Inexpensive
Address: 2018 E Riverside 3
Austin, TX 78741
Phone: (512) 383-5531

#304
Evangeline Café
Cuisines: Cajun, Creole
Average price: Modest
Address: 8106 Brodie Ln
Austin, TX 78745
Phone: (512) 282-2586

#305
Mother's Cafe & Garden
Cuisines: Vegetarian, Vegan
Average price: Modest
Address: 4215 Duval St
Austin, TX 78751
Phone: (512) 451-3994

#306
El Taquito
Cuisines: Mexican
Average price: Inexpensive
Address: 1713 E Riverside Dr
Austin, TX 78741
Phone: (512) 851-8226

#307
East Side King
Cuisines: Asian Fusion, Food Truck
Average price: Modest
Address: 1618 E 6th St
Austin, TX 78702
Phone: (512) 383-8382

#308
Corazon at Castle Hill
Cuisines: Mexican, American
Average price: Modest
Address: 1101 W 5th St
Austin, TX 78703
Phone: (512) 476-0728

Austin Restaurant Guide 2018 / Restaurants, Bars & Cafés

#309
Friends & Neighbors
Cuisines: Café
Average price: Inexpensive
Address: 2614 E Cesar Chavez St
Austin, TX 78702
Phone: (512) 524-1271

#310
Russian House
Cuisines: Russian, Café
Average price: Modest
Address: 307 E 5th St
Austin, TX 78701
Phone: (512) 428-5442

#311
Via 313 Pizza
Cuisines: Pizza
Average price: Modest
Address: 61 Rainey St
Austin, TX 78701
Phone: (512) 609-9405

#312
Cork And Co
Cuisines: Wine Bar, Restaurant
Average price: Modest
Address: 308 Congress Ave
Austin, TX 78703
Phone: (512) 474-2675

#313
Sa-Ten
Cuisines: Japanese, Coffee, Tea
Average price: Modest
Address: 916 Springdale Rd
Austin, TX 78702
Phone: (512) 524-1544

#314
Cherrywood Coffeehouse
Cuisines: Coffee, Tea, Breakfast & Brunch
Average price: Inexpensive
Address: 1400 E 38th 1/2 St
Austin, TX 78722
Phone: (512) 538-1991

#315
Baguette House
Cuisines: Vietnamese, Sandwiches
Average price: Inexpensive
Address: 10901 N Lamar Blvd
Austin, TX 78753
Phone: (512) 837-9100

#316
Pho ThaiSon
Cuisines: Vietnamese
Average price: Inexpensive
Address: 2438 W Anderson Ln
Austin, TX 78757
Phone: (512) 420-0001

#317
Torchy's Tacos
Cuisines: Mexican, Tex-Mex
Average price: Inexpensive
Address: 3005 S Lamar
Austin, TX 78704
Phone: (512) 614-1832

#318
Llama's Peruvian Creole
Cuisines: Street Vendor, Ethnic Food, Peruvian
Average price: Inexpensive
Address: 611 Trinity St
Austin, TX 78701
Phone: (512) 529-4444

#319
Lucy's Fried Chicken
Cuisines: American, Chicken Wings
Average price: Modest
Address: 2218 College Ave
Austin, TX 78704
Phone: (512) 297-2423

#320
Zax Restaurant & Bar
Cuisines: American, Pub
Average price: Modest
Address: 312 Barton Springs Rd
Austin, TX 78704
Phone: (512) 481-0100

#321
Mighty Bird
Cuisines: Breakfast & Brunch, Tex-Mex, American
Average price: Inexpensive
Address: 2900 W Anderson Ln
Austin, TX 78757
Phone: (512) 454-2473

#322
Al Pastor Restaurant & Taco Stand
Cuisines: Mexican
Average price: Inexpensive
Address: 1911 E Riverside
Austin, TX 78741
Phone: (512) 442-8402

Austin Restaurant Guide 2018 / Restaurants, Bars & Cafés

#323
Newk's Eatery
Cuisines: Pizza, Sandwiches, Soup
Average price: Inexpensive
Address: 9722 Great Hills Trl
Austin, TX 78759
Phone: (512) 795-7507

#324
Tom's Tabooley
Cuisines: Middle Eastern, Vegetarian, Mediterranean
Average price: Inexpensive
Address: 2928 Guadalupe St
Austin, TX 78705
Phone: (512) 479-7337

#325
Austin Ale House
Cuisines: Gastropub, American
Average price: Modest
Address: 301 W 6th St
Austin, TX 78701
Phone: (512) 480-9433

#326
Tam Deli & Cafe
Cuisines: Deli, Vietnamese
Average price: Inexpensive
Address: 8222 N Lamar Blvd
Austin, TX 78753
Phone: (512) 834-6458

#327
Tacos Guerrero
Cuisines: Mexican
Average price: Inexpensive
Address: 96 Pleasant Valley Rd
Austin, TX 78702
Phone: (512) 939-2308

#328
Chaat Shop
Cuisines: Indian, Food Truck
Average price: Inexpensive
Address: 1104 E 6th St
Austin, TX 78702
Phone: (512) 660-8507

#329
Ross' Old Austin Cafe
Cuisines: American, Barbeque
Average price: Inexpensive
Address: 11800 N Lamar Blvd
Austin, TX 78753
Phone: (512) 835-2414

#330
Torchy's Tacos
Cuisines: Breakfast & Brunch, Tex-Mex
Average price: Inexpensive
Address: 4301 W William Cannon Dr
Austin, TX 78749
Phone: (512) 514-0767

#331
Chez Zee American Bistro
Cuisines: Desserts, American, Breakfast & Brunch
Average price: Modest
Address: 5406 Balcones Dr
Austin, TX 78731
Phone: (512) 454-2666

#332
Bender Bar & Grill
Cuisines: Lounge, Dive Bar, American
Average price: Inexpensive
Address: 321 W Ben White Blvd
Austin, TX 78798
Phone: (512) 447-1800

#333
Swad
Cuisines: Indian, Vegetarian, Coffee, Tea
Average price: Inexpensive
Address: 9515 N Lamar Blvd
Austin, TX 78753
Phone: (512) 997-7923

#334
Shu Shu's Asian Cuisine
Cuisines: Chinese
Average price: Inexpensive
Address: 8303 Burnet Rd
Austin, TX 78757
Phone: (512) 291-3002

#335
Pacha
Cuisines: Coffee, Tea, Breakfast & Brunch
Average price: Inexpensive
Address: 4618 Burnet Rd
Austin, TX 78756
Phone: (512) 420-8758

#336
The Parlor
Cuisines: Pizza
Average price: Inexpensive
Address: 4301 Guadalupe St
Austin, TX 78751
Phone: (512) 323-0440

Austin Restaurant Guide 2018 / Restaurants, Bars & Cafés

#337
Lone Star BBQ
Cuisines: Food Truck, Barbeque
Average price: Inexpensive
Address: 907 E 6th St
Austin, TX 78702
Phone: (512) 739-4724

#338
Wright Bros Brew & Brew
Cuisines: Bar, Café
Average price: Inexpensive
Address: 500 San Marcos St
Austin, TX 78702
Phone: (512) 493-0963

#339
The Steeping Room
Cuisines: Coffee, Tea, Vegetarian, American
Average price: Modest
Address: 11410 Century Oaks Ter
Austin, TX 78758
Phone: (512) 977-8337

#340
Biscuits and Groovy
Cuisines: Breakfast & Brunch, Food Stand
Average price: Inexpensive
Address: 5015 Duval St
Austin, TX 78751
Phone: (512) 373-6031

#341
Stuffed Cajun Meat Market
Cuisines: Cajun, Creole, Grocery
Average price: Modest
Address: 5207 Brodie Ln
Austin, TX 78745
Phone: (512) 918-1600

#342
The Best Wurst
Cuisines: Food Stand, German, Hot Dogs
Average price: Inexpensive
Address: 201 E 6th St
Austin, TX 78701
Phone: (512) 912-9545

#343
The Frisco
Cuisines: Diner, American, Breakfast & Brunch
Average price: Modest
Address: 6801 Burnet Rd
Austin, TX 78757
Phone: (512) 459-6279

#344
Miguel's The Cubano
Cuisines: Cuban, Street Vendor
Average price: Inexpensive
Address: 611 Trinity St
Austin, TX 78701
Phone: (512) 240-2826

#345
Café Crêpe
Cuisines: Crêperie, French, Breakfast & Brunch
Average price: Inexpensive
Address: 200 San Jacinto Blvd
Austin, TX 78701
Phone: (512) 480-0084

#346
Gregorio's Food Trailer
Cuisines: Food Truck, Italian
Average price: Inexpensive
Address: 1905 S Capital of Texas Hwy
Austin, TX 78746
Phone: (512) 660-7737

#347
Tony's Jamaican Food
Cuisines: Food Stand, Ethnic Food
Average price: Inexpensive
Address: 1200 E 11th St
Austin, TX 78702
Phone: (512) 945-5090

#348
219 West
Cuisines: Bar, American, Event Planning, Service
Average price: Modest
Address: 612 W 6th St
Austin, TX 78701
Phone: (512) 474-2194

#349
Milano Cafe
Cuisines: Italian, European
Average price: Modest
Address: 4601 Southwest Pkwy
Austin, TX 78735
Phone: (512) 428-6076

#350
Snap Kitchen
Cuisines: Gluten-Free, American
Average price: Modest
Address: 1014 W 6th St
Austin, TX 78703
Phone: (512) 479-5959

#351
Snack Bar
Cuisines: American, Wine Bar, Breakfast & Brunch
Average price: Modest
Address: 1224 S Congress Ave
Austin, TX 78704
Phone: (512) 445-2626

#352
Blackbird and Henry
Cuisines: American
Average price: Expensive
Address: 3016 N Guadalupe St
Austin, TX 78705
Phone: (512) 394-5264

#353
Rounders Pizzeria
Cuisines: Pizza
Average price: Modest
Address: 1203 W 6th St
Austin, TX 78703
Phone: (512) 477-0404

#354
Tuk Tuk Thai Café
Cuisines: Thai
Average price: Inexpensive
Address: 5517 Manchaca Rd
Austin, TX 78745
Phone: (512) 326-1619

#355
Dock and Roll Diner
Cuisines: Caterer, Food Stand, Sandwiches
Average price: Modest
Address: 1905 Capital of Texas Hwy
Austin, TX 78746
Phone: (512) 571-2123

#356
Chuy's
Cuisines: Tex-Mex
Average price: Modest
Address: 10520 N Lamar Blvd
Austin, TX 78753
Phone: (512) 836-3218

#357
La Chaparrita
Cuisines: Peruvian, Latin American
Average price: Inexpensive
Address: 6001 Airport Blvd
Austin, TX 78752
Phone: (512) 323-5404

#358
John Mueller Meat Company
Cuisines: Barbeque
Average price: Modest
Address: 2500 E 6th St
Austin, TX 78702
Phone: (512) 524-0559

#359
Terry Black's Barbecue
Cuisines: Barbeque
Average price: Modest
Address: 1003 Barton Springs Rd
Austin, TX 78704
Phone: (512) 394-5899

#360
The Capital Grille
Cuisines: Steakhouse, American
Average price: Expensive
Address: 117 West 4th Street
Austin, TX 78701
Phone: (512) 322-2005

#361
Iron Works Barbecue
Cuisines: Barbeque
Average price: Modest
Address: 100 Red River St
Austin, TX 78701
Phone: (512) 478-4855

#362
Truluck's
Cuisines: Seafood, Steakhouse
Average price: Expensive
Address: 10225 Research Blvd
Austin, TX 78759
Phone: (512) 794-8300

#363
Greek Original Gyros
Cuisines: Greek, Food Truck, Mediterranean
Average price: Inexpensive
Address: 2906 Fruth St
Austin, TX 78705
Phone: (512) 298-9514

#364
Torchy's Tacos
Cuisines: Tex-Mex, Mexican
Average price: Inexpensive
Address: 5119 Burnet Rd
Austin, TX 78756
Phone: (512) 382-0823

Austin Restaurant Guide 2018 / Restaurants, Bars & Cafés

#365
Lucy's Fried Chicken
Cuisines: American
Average price: Modest
Address: 5408 Burnet Rd
Austin, TX 78756
Phone: (512) 514-0664

#366
Unity Vegan Kitchen
Cuisines: Food Truck, Vegan
Average price: Inexpensive
Address: 415 Jessie St
Austin, TX 78704
Phone: (972) 345-4990

#367
Cypress Grill
Cuisines: American, Cajun, Creole
Average price: Modest
Address: 4404 W William Cannon Dr
Austin, TX 78749
Phone: (512) 358-7474

#368
Kesos Taco House
Cuisines: Tex-Mex, Mexican
Average price: Inexpensive
Address: 4720 S Congress Ave
Austin, TX 78745
Phone: (512) 358-4555

#369
Mellizoz Tacos
Cuisines: Tex-Mex, Food Truck
Average price: Inexpensive
Address: 1503 S 1st St
Austin, TX 78704
Phone: (512) 916-4996

#370
La Condesa
Cuisines: Mexican
Average price: Expensive
Address: 400 W 2nd St
Austin, TX 78701
Phone: (512) 499-0300

#371
Phara's
Cuisines: Mediterranean, Hookah Bar
Average price: Modest
Address: 111 E N Loop Blvd
Austin, TX 78751
Phone: (512) 632-7067

#372
Trudy's
Cuisines: Tex-Mex, Bar
Average price: Modest
Address: 409 W 30th St
Austin, TX 78705
Phone: (512) 477-2935

#373
Live Oak Barbecue & Beer
Cuisines: Barbeque
Average price: Modest
Address: 2713 E 2nd St
Austin, TX 78702
Phone: (512) 524-1930

#374
Sweet Ritual
Cuisines: Vegan, Ice Cream
Average price: Inexpensive
Address: 4500 Duval St
Austin, TX 78751
Phone: (512) 666-8346

#375
Stubb's Bar-B-Q
Cuisines: Barbeque
Average price: Modest
Address: 801 Red River St
Austin, TX 78701
Phone: (512) 480-8341

#376
Tortilleria Rio Grande
Cuisines: Mexican
Average price: Inexpensive
Address: 900 E Braker Ln
Austin, TX 78753
Phone: (512) 973-9696

#377
Sushi Junai
Cuisines: Sushi Bar, Japanese
Average price: Modest
Address: 1612 Lavaca St
Austin, TX 78701
Phone: (512) 322-2428

#378
El Regio
Cuisines: Mexican
Average price: Inexpensive
Address: 1725 Ohlen Rd
Austin, TX 78757
Phone: (512) 323-0044

#379
Soco Burgers
Cuisines: Burgers, Food Stand
Average price: Inexpensive
Address: 2400 S Congress Ave
Austin, TX 78704
Phone: (512) 445-7121

#380
Mom's Taste
Cuisines: Korean, Grocery
Average price: Inexpensive
Address: 6613 Airport Blvd
Austin, TX 78752
Phone: (512) 420-0499

#381
Alta's Cafe
Cuisines: Coffee, Tea, Café
Average price: Modest
Address: 74 Trinity St
Austin, TX 78701
Phone: (512) 499-0470

#382
Curra's Grill
Cuisines: Mexican
Average price: Modest
Address: 614 E Oltorf St
Austin, TX 78704
Phone: (512) 444-0012

#383
Dumpling Happiness
Cuisines: Food Truck, Chinese, Street Vendor
Average price: Inexpensive
Address: 1816 E 6th St.
Austin, TX 78702
Phone: (512) 609-0186

#384
Taverna
Cuisines: Italian
Average price: Modest
Address: 258 W 2nd St
Austin, TX 78701
Phone: (512) 477-1001

#385
Counter Cafe
Cuisines: Diner, Café
Average price: Modest
Address: 626 N Lamar Blvd
Austin, TX 78703
Phone: (512) 708-8800

#386
Smashburger
Cuisines: Burgers
Average price: Inexpensive
Address: 1200 Barbara Jordan Blvd
Austin, TX 78723
Phone: (512) 872-2926

#387
Upstairs on Trinity
Cuisines: Tapas, Champagne Bar, Wine Bar
Average price: Modest
Address: 607 Trinity St
Austin, TX 78701
Phone: (512) 358-6202

#388
Mai Thai Restaurant
Cuisines: Thai, Bar
Average price: Modest
Address: 207 San Jacinto Blvd
Austin, TX 78701
Phone: (512) 482-8244

#389
Daruma Ramen
Cuisines: Ramen
Average price: Modest
Address: 612-B E 6th St
Austin, TX 78701
Phone: (512) 369-3897

#390
Tyson's Tacos
Cuisines: Mexican
Average price: Inexpensive
Address: 4905 Airport Blvd
Austin, TX 78751
Phone: (512) 451-3326

#391
Cover 3
Cuisines: American, Sports Bar
Average price: Modest
Address: 2700 W Anderson Ln
Austin, TX 78757
Phone: (512) 374-1121

#392
Pleasant Storage Room
Cuisines: Cocktail Bar, Caribbean, Tapas
Average price: Modest
Address: 208 W 4th St
Austin, TX 78701
Phone: (512) 322-9921

#393
Ken's Subs Tacos & More
Cuisines: Sandwiches, Mexican
Average price: Inexpensive
Address: 9408 Dessau Rd
Austin, TX 78754
Phone: (512) 837-9370

#394
Coco's Cafe
Cuisines: Taiwanese, Coffee, Tea
Average price: Inexpensive
Address: 8557 Research Blvd Ste 118
Austin, TX 78758
Phone: (512) 833-6588

#395
P. Terry's
Cuisines: American, Burgers
Average price: Inexpensive
Address: 3303 N Lamar Blvd
Austin, TX 78705
Phone: (512) 371-9975

#396
Jalapeño's Taco Bar
Cuisines: Mexican, Burgers
Average price: Inexpensive
Address: 6002 Burleson Rd
Austin, TX 78744
Phone: (512) 326-1213

#397
Wahoo's Fish Tacos
Cuisines: Mexican, Seafood
Average price: Inexpensive
Address: 509-A Rio Grande St.
Austin, TX 78701
Phone: (512) 476-3474

#398
Kerbey Lane Cafe Westlake
Cuisines: American, Breakfast & Brunch
Average price: Modest
Address: 701 S. Capital of Texas Hwy
Austin, TX 78746
Phone: (512) 879-2820

#399
Fresa's
Cuisines: Mexican
Average price: Modest
Address: 915 N Lamar Blvd
Austin, TX 78703
Phone: (512) 428-5077

#400
Arirang Restaurant
Cuisines: Korean
Average price: Modest
Address: 6801 Airport Blvd
Austin, TX 78752
Phone: (512) 454-6364

#401
Tacodeli
Cuisines: Tex-Mex, Mexican
Average price: Inexpensive
Address: 7301 Burnet Rd
Austin, TX 78757
Phone: (512) 467-9999

#402
Bufalo Bob's Chalupa Wagon
Cuisines: Food Stand, Gluten-Free, Tex-Mex
Average price: Inexpensive
Address: 411 W 23rd
Austin, TX 78705
Phone: (512) 662-2801

#403
Hoover's Cooking
Cuisines: Southern, American
Average price: Modest
Address: 2002 Manor Rd
Austin, TX 78722
Phone: (512) 479-5006

#404
Burger Tex 2
Cuisines: Burgers
Average price: Inexpensive
Address: 2912 Guadalupe St
Austin, TX 78705
Phone: (512) 477-8433

#405
Bar-B-Q Heaven
Cuisines: Barbeque
Average price: Inexpensive
Address: 519 East 7th Street
Austin, TX 78701
Phone: (512) 299-7461

#406
D K Sushi & Seoul Asian Food Market
Cuisines: Grocery, Sushi Bar
Average price: Modest
Address: 5610 N Lamar Blvd
Austin, TX 78751
Phone: (512) 302-1090

#407
Chapli Kababs n Curries
Cuisines: Indian, Afghan, Pakistani
Average price: Modest
Address: 1200 W Howard Ln
Austin, TX 78753
Phone: (512) 989-2928

#408
Lulu B's
Cuisines: Vietnamese, Food Stand
Average price: Inexpensive
Address: 2113 S Lamar Blvd
Austin, TX 78704
Phone: (512) 921-4828

#409
The Grove
Cuisines: Wine Bar, American
Average price: Modest
Address: 3001 RR 620 S
Austin, TX 78738
Phone: (512) 263-2366

#410
El Tacorrido
Cuisines: Mexican
Average price: Inexpensive
Address: 9320 N Lamar Blvd
Austin, TX 78753
Phone: (512) 873-8602

#411
Red's Porch
Cuisines: Southern, Cajun, Creole, Tex-Mex
Average price: Modest
Address: 3508 S Lamar Blvd
Austin, TX 78704
Phone: (512) 440-7337

#412
**Agazajo's Flying Pizza
& Italian Restaurant**
Cuisines: Italian, Pizza
Average price: Modest
Address: 2406 Us Hwy 183 S
Austin, TX 78744
Phone: (512) 389-2558

#413
Titaya's Thai Cuisine
Cuisines: Thai
Average price: Modest
Address: 5501 N Lamar Blvd
Austin, TX 78751
Phone: (512) 458-1792

#414
Shiner's Saloon
Cuisines: Bar, American, Music Venues
Average price: Inexpensive
Address: 422 Congress Ave
Austin, TX 78701
Phone: (512) 448-4600

#415
Vazquez Restaurant
Cuisines: Mexican
Average price: Inexpensive
Address: 9063 Research Blvd
Austin, TX 78758
Phone: (512) 832-9956

#416
Asia Cafe
Cuisines: Chinese
Average price: Inexpensive
Address: 8650 Spicewood Springs Rd,
Ste 114A Austin, TX 78759
Phone: (512) 331-5788

#417
Black Walnut Café
Cuisines: Café, American,
Breakfast & Brunch
Average price: Modest
Address: 10817 Ranch Road 2222
Austin, TX 78730
Phone: (512) 241-0333

#418
Texas Cuban
Cuisines: Cuban, Food Stand
Average price: Inexpensive
Address: 1700 S Lamar Ave
Austin, TX 78704
Phone: (512) 294-9259

#419
34th Street Cafe
Cuisines: American, Caterer
Average price: Modest
Address: 1005 W 34th St
Austin, TX 78705
Phone: (512) 371-3400

#420
Cipollina
Cuisines: Italian
Average price: Modest
Address: 1213 W Lynn St
Austin, TX 78703
Phone: (512) 477-5211

#421
Chez Nous
Cuisines: French
Average price: Expensive
Address: 510 Neches St
Austin, TX 78701
Phone: (512) 473-2413

#422
Shawarma Point
Cuisines: Halal, Food Stand, Middle Eastern
Average price: Inexpensive
Address: 519 E 7th St
Austin, TX 78701
Phone: (512) 887-0076

#423
El Naranjo
Cuisines: Mexican
Average price: Expensive
Address: 85 Rainey St
Austin, TX 78701
Phone: (512) 474-2776

#424
Winflo Osteria
Cuisines: Pizza, Italian
Average price: Modest
Address: 1315 W 6th St
Austin, TX 78703
Phone: (512) 582-1027

#425
Freddie's Place
Cuisines: American
Average price: Inexpensive
Address: 1703 S 1st St
Austin, TX 78704
Phone: (512) 445-9197

#426
The Original New Orleans Po-Boy and Gumbo Shop III
Cuisines: Cajun, Creole, Food Stand
Average price: Inexpensive
Address: 11 W 23rd St
Austin, TX 78705
Phone: (512) 406-9237

#427
Habesha Ethiopian Restaurant & Bar
Cuisines: Ethiopian
Average price: Modest
Address: 6019 IH 35 N
Austin, TX 78723
Phone: (512) 358-6839

#428
The Pizza Shop
Cuisines: Pizza
Average price: Inexpensive
Address: 1906 S 1st St
Austin, TX 78704
Phone: (512) 373-2937

#429
Cow Tipping Creamery
Cuisines: Desserts, Ice Cream, American
Average price: Inexpensive
Address: 2512 Rio Grande
Austin, TX 78705
Phone: (512) 538-4039

#430
Toastie's Sub Shop
Cuisines: Deli, Sandwiches
Average price: Inexpensive
Address: 215 S Lamar Blvd
Austin, TX 78704
Phone: (512) 499-8500

#431
Man Bites Dog
Cuisines: Hot Dogs
Average price: Inexpensive
Address: 5222 Burnet Rd
Austin, TX 78756
Phone: (512) 614-1330

#432
Flour and Vine
Cuisines: American
Average price: Modest
Address: 300 S Lamar Blvd
Austin, TX 78704
Phone: (512) 474-4846

#433
Sichuan River
Cuisines: Szechuan
Average price: Modest
Address: 4534 W Gate Blvd
Austin, TX 78745
Phone: (512) 892-6699

#434
Rudy's Country Store & Barbecue
Cuisines: Barbeque, Gas & Service Station
Average price: Modest
Address: 11570 Research Blvd
Austin, TX 78759
Phone: (512) 418-9898

Austin Restaurant Guide 2018 / Restaurants, Bars & Cafés

#435
First Wok
Cuisines: Chinese
Average price: Inexpensive
Address: 603 W Stassney Ln
Austin, TX 78745
Phone: (512) 444-0077

#436
Ranch 616
Cuisines: American
Average price: Modest
Address: 616 Nueces St
Austin, TX 78701
Phone: (512) 479-7616

#437
East Side Pies Too!
Cuisines: Pizza
Average price: Modest
Address: 5312 Airport Blvd
Austin, TX 78751
Phone: (512) 454-7437

#438
Phil's Icehouse
Cuisines: Burgers
Average price: Inexpensive
Address: 5620 Burnet Rd
Austin, TX 78756
Phone: (512) 524-1212

#439
WuWu Sushi
Cuisines: Sushi Bar, Asian Fusion
Average price: Modest
Address: 1407 E 7th St
Austin, TX 78702
Phone: (512) 828-6919

#440
The Steeping Room
Cuisines: Coffee, Tea, Vegetarian, Gluten-Free
Average price: Modest
Address: 4400 N Lamar Blvd
Austin, TX 78756
Phone: (512) 467-2663

#441
Culver's
Cuisines: American, Burgers
Average price: Inexpensive
Address: 2240 W Braker Ln
Austin, TX 78758
Phone: (512) 836-4162

#442
Tex-Mex Joe's
Cuisines: Tex-Mex, Mexican
Average price: Inexpensive
Address: 7600 N Lamar Blvd
Austin, TX 78752
Phone: (512) 371-3625

#443
El Chilito
Cuisines: Mexican
Average price: Inexpensive
Address: 2219 Manor Dr
Austin, TX 78722
Phone: (512) 382-3797

#444
Thai Fresh
Cuisines: Thai
Average price: Modest
Address: 909 W Mary St
Austin, TX 78704
Phone: (512) 494-6436

#445
Mi Pizza
Cuisines: Pizza, Vegan
Average price: Inexpensive
Address: 6001 W Parmer Ln
Austin, TX 78727
Phone: (512) 258-5700

#446
Shabu
Cuisines: Hot Pot, Chinese
Average price: Modest
Address: 2700 Anderson Ln
Austin, TX 78757
Phone: (512) 336-8888

#447
Chinatown
Cuisines: Sushi Bar, Dim Sum
Average price: Modest
Address: 2712 Bee Cave Rd
Austin, TX 78746
Phone: (512) 328-6588

#448
Zocalo Café
Cuisines: Mexican
Average price: Modest
Address: 1110 W Lynn
Austin, TX 78703
Phone: (512) 472-8226

#449
Milto's
Cuisines: Pizza, Greek, Mediterranean
Average price: Inexpensive
Address: 2909 Guadalupe St
Austin, TX 78705
Phone: (512) 476-1021

#450
Donut Taco Palace III
Cuisines: Donuts, Fast Food, Mexican
Average price: Inexpensive
Address: 6214 N Lamar Blvd
Austin, TX 78752
Phone: (512) 374-9527

#451
Giovanni's Pizza Stand
Cuisines: Pizza, Food Stand
Average price: Inexpensive
Address: 2900 B S Lamar Blvd
Austin, TX 78704
Phone: (512) 442-7033

#452
El Meson
Cuisines: Mexican
Average price: Inexpensive
Address: 5808 Burleson Rd
Austin, TX 78744
Phone: (512) 416-0749

#453
Eden East
Cuisines: American, Farmers Market
Average price: Exclusive
Address: 755 Springdale Rd
Austin, TX 78702
Phone: (512) 428-6500

#454
Taqueria Guadalajara
Cuisines: Mexican, Breakfast & Brunch
Average price: Inexpensive
Address: 6534 Burnet Rd
Austin, TX 78757
Phone: (512) 452-9886

#455
Piranha Killer Sushi
Cuisines: Sushi Bar
Average price: Modest
Address: 207 San Jacinto Blvd
Austin, TX 78701
Phone: (512) 473-8775

#456
Nasha
Cuisines: Indian
Average price: Modest
Address: 1614 E 7th St
Austin, TX 78702
Phone: (512) 350-2919

#457
Torchy's Tacos
Cuisines: Tex-Mex, Mexican, Breakfast & Brunch
Average price: Inexpensive
Address: 11521 Ranch Rd 620 N
Austin, TX 78726
Phone: (512) 381-8226

#458
PhoNatic
Cuisines: Vietnamese
Average price: Inexpensive
Address: 2525 W Anderson Ln
Austin, TX 78757
Phone: (512) 458-8889

#459
Mandola's Italian Market
Cuisines: Italian, Grocery
Average price: Modest
Address: 4700 W Guadalupe St
Austin, TX 78751
Phone: (512) 419-9700

#460
Black Sheep Lodge
Cuisines: Pub, Burgers, Hot Dogs
Average price: Modest
Address: 2108 S Lamar Blvd
Austin, TX 78704
Phone: (512) 707-2744

#461
La Mexicana Bakery
Cuisines: Bakery, Mexican, Desserts
Average price: Inexpensive
Address: 1924 S 1st St
Austin, TX 78704
Phone: (512) 443-6369

#462
Russell's Bistro
Cuisines: Breakfast & Brunch, American
Average price: Modest
Address: 1601 W 38th St
Austin, TX 78731
Phone: (512) 467-7877

#463
Leaf
Cuisines: American
Average price: Modest
Address: 419 W 2nd St
Austin, TX 78701
Phone: (512) 474-5323

#464
Maudie's Café
Cuisines: Tex-Mex, Breakfast & Brunch
Average price: Inexpensive
Address: 2608 W 7th St
Austin, TX 78703
Phone: (512) 473-3740

#465
Halal Bros
Cuisines: Halal, Food Stand
Average price: Inexpensive
Address: 419 E 7th St
Austin, TX 78701
Phone: (512) 284-8105

#466
Cazamance
Cuisines: Food Stand, African
Average price: Inexpensive
Address: 1308 East 4th St
Austin, TX 78704
Phone: (512) 769-9560

#467
Snap Kitchen
Cuisines: Gluten-Free, American, Juice Bar
Average price: Modest
Address: 4616 Triangle Ave
Austin, TX 78751
Phone: (512) 459-9000

#468
Kismet Cafe
Cuisines: Greek, Middle Eastern, Mediterranean
Average price: Inexpensive
Address: 411 W 24th St
Austin, TX 78705
Phone: (512) 236-1811

#469
Nau's Enfield Drug
Cuisines: Drugstore, Ice Cream, Burgers
Average price: Inexpensive
Address: 1115 W Lynn St
Austin, TX 78703
Phone: (512) 476-1221

#470
In-N-Out Burger
Cuisines: Burgers, Fast Food
Average price: Inexpensive
Address: 4508 I-35 N
Austin, TX 78751
Phone: (800) 786-1000

#471
Messhall Cafe
Cuisines: Breakfast & Brunch, American
Average price: Inexpensive
Address: 1019 Brazos St
Austin, TX 78701
Phone: (512) 322-9625

#472
South Austin Trailer Park & Eatery
Cuisines: Food Stand, Tex-Mex, Mexican
Average price: Inexpensive
Address: 1311 S 1st St
Austin, TX 78704
Phone: (512) 366-0537

#473
Hot Rod Coffee Trailer
Cuisines: Coffee, Tea, Food Stand
Average price: Inexpensive
Address: 6546 Burnet Rd
Austin, TX 78757
Phone: (512) 516-3113

#474
County Line On The Lake
Cuisines: Barbeque
Average price: Modest
Address: 5204 Ranch Road 2222
Austin, TX 78731
Phone: (512) 346-3664

#475
Hai Ky
Cuisines: Vietnamese, Asian Fusion
Average price: Modest
Address: 3736 Bee Caves Rd
Austin, TX 78798
Phone: (512) 732-2005

#476
Malaga
Cuisines: Tapas Bar, Spanish
Average price: Modest
Address: 440 W 2nd St
Austin, TX 78701
Phone: (512) 236-8020

#477
Biryani Pot
Cuisines: Indian
Average price: Modest
Address: 12407 N Mopac Expy
Austin, TX 78758
Phone: (512) 837-4444

#478
BD Riley's Irish Pub & Restaurant
Cuisines: Pub, Irish
Average price: Modest
Address: 204 E 6th St
Austin, TX 78701
Phone: (512) 494-1335

#479
Cedar Door
Cuisines: Bar, American
Average price: Modest
Address: 201 Brazos St
Austin, TX 78701
Phone: (512) 473-3712

#480
Bombay Bistro
Cuisines: Indian
Average price: Modest
Address: 4200 S Lamar Blvd
Austin, TX 78704
Phone: (512) 462-7227

#481
Estancia Churrascaria
Cuisines: Steakhouse, Brazilian
Average price: Expensive
Address: 10000 Research Blvd
Austin, TX 78759
Phone: (512) 345-5600

#482
Fat Sal's
Cuisines: Hot Dogs, Burgers, Sandwiches
Average price: Modest
Address: 2604 Guadalupe St
Austin, TX 78705
Phone: (855) 682-4373

#483
Takoba
Cuisines: Mexican, Lounge
Average price: Modest
Address: 1411 E 7th St
Austin, TX 78702
Phone: (512) 628-4466

#484
Maudie's Milagro
Cuisines: Tex-Mex
Average price: Modest
Address: 3801 N Capital of Texas Hwy
Austin, TX 78746
Phone: (512) 306-8080

#485
BBQ Revolution
Cuisines: Food Truck, Vegan
Average price: Inexpensive
Address: 3111 Manor Rd
Austin, TX 78723
Phone: (512) 584-7659

#486
Texas French Bread
Cuisines: Bakery, Sandwiches, American
Average price: Modest
Address: 2900 Rio Grande St
Austin, TX 78705
Phone: (512) 499-0544

#487
Jalapeños Taco Bar
Cuisines: Mexican, Tex-Mex
Average price: Inexpensive
Address: 3518 E 7th St
Austin, TX 78702
Phone: (512) 386-5013

#488
GreenGos
Cuisines: Salad
Average price: Inexpensive
Address: 1200 Barbara Jordan Blvd
Austin, TX 78722
Phone: (512) 499-1565

#489
Pho Van
Cuisines: Vietnamese
Average price: Inexpensive
Address: 8557 Research Blvd
Austin, TX 78758
Phone: (512) 832-5595

#490
Ramos Restaurant
Cuisines: Tex-Mex, Mexican
Average price: Inexpensive
Address: 14611 N Mopac Expy
Austin, TX 78728
Phone: (512) 246-0727

#491
Opal Divine's Davenport
Cuisines: Restaurant
Average price: Modest
Address: 3801 N Capital of Texas Hwy
Austin, TX 78746
Phone: (512) 369-3709

#492
Casa Chapala
Cuisines: Mexican
Average price: Modest
Address: 9041 Research Blvd
Austin, TX 78758
Phone: (512) 459-4242

#493
Trudy's
Cuisines: Tex-Mex, Bar
Average price: Modest
Address: 901 Little Texas Ln
Austin, TX 78745
Phone: (512) 326-9899

#494
G'Raj Mahal Cafe & Lounge
Cuisines: Indian, Vegetarian
Average price: Modest
Address: 73 Rainey Street
Austin, TX 78701
Phone: (512) 480-2255

#495
Threadgill's
Cuisines: Southern, Music Venues
Average price: Modest
Address: 301 W Riverside Dr
Austin, TX 78704
Phone: (512) 472-9304

#496
Ruby's Barbeque & Catering
Cuisines: Barbeque
Average price: Modest
Address: 512 W 29th St
Austin, TX 78705
Phone: (512) 477-1651

#497
East Side Pies
Cuisines: Pizza
Average price: Modest
Address: 1809 W Anderson Ln
Austin, TX 78757
Phone: (512) 467-8900

#498
Noodles and Company
Cuisines: American, Mediterranean, Asian Fusion
Average price: Inexpensive
Address: 3300 Bee Caves Rd
Austin, TX 78746
Phone: (512) 329-5923

#499
Fry Baby
Cuisines: American, Fish & Chips, Food Truck
Average price: Inexpensive
Address: 343 S. Congress
Austin, TX 78704
Phone: (512) 800-4647

#500
Cafe Mueller
Cuisines: Café
Average price: Inexpensive
Address: 1801 E 51st St
Austin, TX 78723
Phone: (512) 474-2199